Raspberry PI3

Enchanted Guide for Starters

Thomas Charleston

Contents

1.
What is the Raspberry Pi 3?

Raspberry Pi is a little credit card-sized computer that connects to your TV or monitor. It is very powerful yet small device that allows people of all ages to explore the world of computers and learn how to program in languages such as Python and Scratch. The device is capable of doing absolutely everything you expect from an ordinary desktop computer, from the Internet search and playing HD videos to creating tables, processing of voice and gaming. Even more so, Raspberry Pi has the ability to interact with the outside world. It has been used in a wide field of making digital projects, from musical instruments and detectors for parents to the meteorological stations and homes for birds with infra-red cameras. Image 1 shows Raspberry Pi 3 device.

Image 1: Raspberry Pi 3

1.1. Specification

The Raspberry Pi 3 is the third generation of Raspberry Pi. The main differences with the previous model are [1]:

- 1.2GHz 64-bit quad-core ARMv8 CPU
- 802.11n Wireless LAN
- Bluetooth 4.1
- Bluetooth Low Energy (BLE)

Other components are:

- 1GB RAM
- 4 USB Ports
- 40 GPIO pins
- Full HDMI port
- Ethernet port
- Combined 3.5mm audio jack with composite video
- Camera interface (CSI)
- Display interface (DSI)
- Micro SD card slot
- VideoCore IV 3D graphics core

1.2. Operating systems

In order to use the device, operating system is required. Choosing the operating system can seem like hard work, however, the best approach is to choose a system that suits the needs of the task. If you are a beginner, the best operating system for playing with the device is Raspbian. In the table below we can see a couple of the most popular operating systems that are customized for the Raspberry Pi.

Operating system (OS)	Logo	Description
Raspbian		Raspbian is the official supported operating system.
Pidora		Pidora is Fedora Remix operating system optimized to work with Raspberry Pi
RaspBMC		OSMC is a free and open source media center
OpenELEC		OpenELEC is a small Linux based OS that turns your computer into a Kodi media center.
RISC OS		RISCOS operating system is very fast and compact, and is specially designed for devices with ARM architecture.
Arch		Arch represents a lightweight and flexible Linux distribution

Table 1: The most popular operating systems for Raspberry Pi 3

1.3. Raspbian

Raspbian is the most popular operating system used on Raspberry Pi devices. It is completely free and it is based on Debian. It represents set of programs and utilities that makes sure your device is running properly. Raspbian isn't just an operating system, it comes also with over 35,000 packages in a format suitable for quick installation. Raspbian operating system is improving daily and is still under active development. The operating system comes with a desktop environment that is made to look like operating systems we use every day. In addition to the menu at the top left corner, in the upper right corner, tape with active programs is located. Using the desktop environment is perfect for users who are not dealing well with the Linux console. It is important to remember that the mere specification of Raspberry Pi 3 device is not strong enough for some big processes we use on desktop computers, such as watching 4K movies, video editing and photography. Given that the Raspbian is Linux distribution, it has very good security features as well as excellent networking capabilities.

2.
How to set up Raspberry Pi 3?

Device setup is very simple and can be completed in less than an hour. The table below shows the components required for initial setup of the device.

Name	Image	Comment	Quantity
Raspberry Pi 3		Single board computer	1
Mouse		Requires mouse with USB connection	1
Keyboard		Requires keyboard with USB connection	1
Micro SD card		At least 4 GB, 8 GB recommended	1
Ethernet cable		Cable longer than 1m is recommended for ease of moving the	1

		device	
MicroUSB Charger		If you connect devices that require more power, such as internet modem, it is necessary to use a stronger charger, at least 2A	1
HDMI cable		Cable longer than 1m is recommended for ease of moving the device	1
Monitor		Support for HDMI is required	1

Table 2: Components required for initial setup of the Raspberry Pi 3

Connecting all components is very simple and does not differ from connecting normal computers. Before connecting all components, it is necessary to install the operating system on the Micro SD card. Given that this is guide for the beginners, we will be showing the installation of the Raspbian operating system.

2.1. Installing Raspbian on Micro SD card

The latest version of Raspbian is Jessie. There are two versions of Raspbian operating system, complete Raspbian Jessie with Pixel and minified Jessie Lite. The difference between those two versions is that the Lite version comes with a minimum number of pre-installed packages and therefore it is of 1 GB less than the full version. A minified version is suitable for servers, because there is no support for the Desktop or Bluetooth, however, there is a possibility of subsequent installation of additional packages.

A few steps to install the operating system:

• Download last Raspbian image (Jessie) from official page https://www.raspberrypi.org/downloads/raspbian/

• After downloading .zip file, unzip it to get image file (.img)

• In order to record an operating system on the card, we need a program to write files, an image writing tool.

• Raspberry Pi documentation recommends Win32DiskImager utility for Windows users. Download and install it from https://sourceforge.net/projects/win32diskimager/

• Insert Micro SD cart to your computer via SD card reader or you can use SD adapter and USB port.

• Check the drive letter assigned to the memory card, for example "G:".

• Install and Run Win32DiskImager that was previously downloaded and run it as administrator by right clicking on executable file and choosing option "Run as administrator".

• When Win32DiskImager opens choose the image file (.img) that we extracted in step two.

• Select the drive letter assigned to Micro SD card. Be careful when selecting the drive, because selecting the wrong drive can cause loss of data.

• Click on write button, and wait for process to complete.

• Close Win32DiskImager and eject Micro SD card.

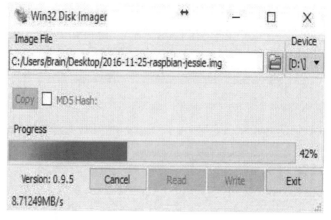

Image 2: Win32 Disk Imager user interface

If you are using Mac OS or Linux, check this link: *https://www.raspberrypi.org/documentation/installation/installing-images/*

However, there are two ways to set up Raspberry Pi 3:

• The usual way

• Connecting via SSH protocol

2.2. The usual way to set up

Make sure that all the devices listed in Table 1 are connected and that the Micro SD card is inserted. Plug the charger into an outlet and the device will automatically turn on and it will start the boot process. If everything is connected correctly, red light should be on continuously and the green periodically. The red light indicates that the device is supplied with power and the green light represents reading from a memory card. There are two more LEDs at the Ethernet port, green and red, which indicates whether or not device is connected to network and network speed.

Depending on the version of the operating system, the system can be launched in console or desktop environment. In the event that the system is running in console, sign in is required. Default Raspberry Pi credentials are **"pi"** for username and "raspberry" for password. Opening desktop environment is done by typing the command **"startx"**.

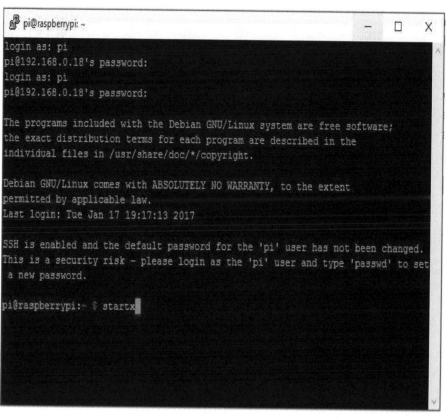

Image 3: Starting Desktop environment from CLI with "startx" command

In case we want to change from desktop environment to console, we can do it simply by clicking menu and choosing shutdown option. In shutdown window all we need to do is to choose exit to command line.

2.3. Connecting via SSH protocol

In case you want to set the device through SSH protocol, you need fewer components than shown in Table 1. Components you need:

- Raspberry Pi 3
- Ethernet cable
- Charger
- Micro SD card with pre-installed operating system

As in the previous case, it is necessary to check whether all of the above devices are connected and that the Micro SD card is inserted. Given that now we do not connect the monitor, it is necessary to pay attention to the LEDs. When all the lights turn on and light as indicated in the previous case, it is necessary to wait for 30 seconds to one minute, so that the device has time to connect to the network. Once it is connected to network, we need to find out IP address of Raspberry Pi. The easiest way to find out the IP address of the device is scanning the network. Network scanning is a simple process, and it is easiest to accomplish it using the Advanced IP Scanner program. Program is completely free and can be downloaded from the official website *http://www.advanced-ip-scanner.com/*. Once you download it, you need to install it. Follow the install instructions and after the installation is finished, run the program. In the top left corner of the screen there is a "Scan" button with the green arrow. Push the button and wait for scanning process to be finished. Number of found devices depends on how big your network is. If it is a small home network, you should find a couple devices on the list, which makes it easier to find Raspberry Pi device. Table in which devices are listed contains several columns, such as status, name, IP address, manufacturer, MAC address. In the table we need to find a device whose manufacturer is Raspberry Pi Foundation. Just next to the manufacturer, the IP address of the device is located.

When we have determined an IP address of the device, the next step is to connect. To connect to Raspberry Pi remotely we need an SSH client. One of the best SSH clients is PuTTy. It is very lightweight and easy to install and of course completely free. You can find it and download it from official website *http://www.chiark.greenend.org.uk/~sgtatham/putty/downlo ad.html.* When you download the program, install it and run it.

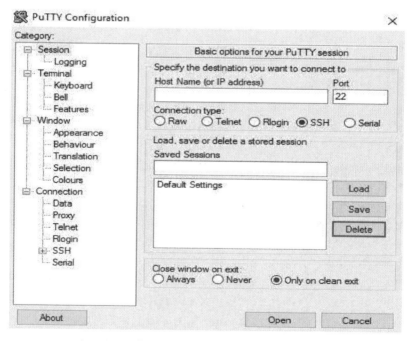

Image 4: The appearance of SSH client PuTTY

In Host Name field, we should enter the IP address that we have previously found using the Advanced IP Scanner. Port should remain the same because 22 is default port for SSH protocol. Once we entered IP address, click "Open" button. If the connection is successful, we will get a black screen on which we will be asked to sign in. Username and password are default ones like in previous setup scenario. Username is "pi" and password is **"raspberry"**.

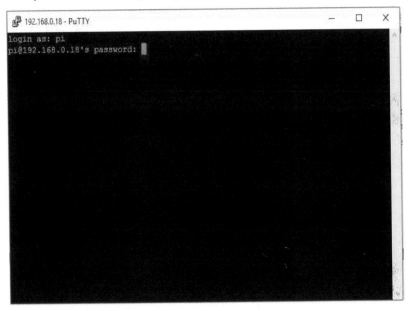

Image 5: Login via SSH

2.4. Root user and sudo

Linux operating system supports multiple users, thus different users have different roles. And different roles have different privileges. Most users can run most programs, as well as read and edit most of the files in your folders. But one user can't change or access data from another user. But there is special user in Linux known as superuser, which usually have the username root and it has unrestricted access to computer and can do almost anything.

You can use "sudo" command to provide access as super user. When logged in as a normal user, using the username "pi", we do not have full access. However, by using "sudo" before the command we want to execute, we have then full access. If we want to install additional software, we normally use apt-get. To update the list of available software, you need to prefix the apt-get command with "sudo":

```
sudo apt-get update
```

More about the apt-get commands you can read in the text below.

It would substantially undermine the security of the operating system if everyone had the ability to act as a superuser. Users who can use the "sudo" command we call sudoers. User "pi" is included in sudoers list by default. To allow other users to act as superuser, we can add them to "sudo" group with usermod, edit the /etc/sudoers.

2.5. Commands apt-get update and apt-get upgrade

After downloading and installing the system it is always recommended to update and upgrade the operating system. We can update our system`s package list by entering next command:

```
sudo apt-get update
```

After update, it is recommended to upgrade system by entering following command:

```
sudo apt-get upgrade
```

Depending on the version of the installed operating system and few other factors like internet speed, executing these commands might take some time.

2.6. Command raspi-config

Command raspi-config represents Raspberry Pi configuration tool. To open configuration tool type in following command:

```
sudo raspi-conifg
```

Command sudo is required because we might change files that don't belong to us, from user perspective. On image 6 we can see look of configuration tool.

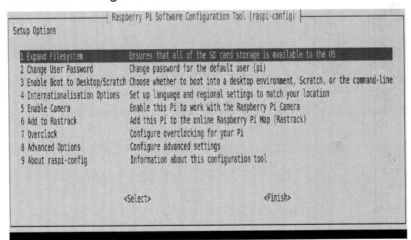

Image 6: Raspberry Pi – Configuration tool

Raspberry Pi configuration tool has following options:

• **Expand Filesystem** - Ensures that all of the SD card storage is available to the OS

• **Change User Password** - Change password for the default user (pi)

- **Enable Boot to Desktop/Scratch** - Choose whether to boot into a desktop environment, Scratch, or the command line

- **Internationalization Options** - Set up language and regional settings to match your location

- **Enable Camera** - Enable this Pi to work with the Raspberry Pi camera

- **Add to Rastrack** - Add this Pi to the online Raspberry Pi Map (Rastrack)

- **Overclock** - Configure overclocking for your Pi

- **Advanced Options** - Configure advanced settings

- **About raspi-config** - Information about this configuration tool

Inside configuration tool window we use *up* and *down* keys to navigate. When we press *right* arrow key we will exit to footer section where we can choose between *<Select>* and *<Finish>*. We can use *Tab* button to switch between these sections (list and footer). Command *raspi-config* provides functionality to make configurations changes. Some options may require system reboot. When we are done with changes, we should press *<Finish>* button. Below we will explain in more detail some of the options that are commonly used.

2.6.1. Expend Filesystem

When we install Raspbian on our Micro SD card, then a portion of memory card will be unused. Selecting this option will increase the place on the memory card that we can use for our files or programs. No confirmation will be displayed after clicking this option it will automatically expand file system. Note that reboot is required for changes to take place.

2.6.2. Enable boot to Desktop or Scratch

Here we can choose what happens when the device boots. This option is also available from the Desktop environment.

2.6.3. Enable camera

In case we want to use the camera we have to enable this option. If this option is enabled, it ensures that the at least 128MB of RAM is dedicated to GPU.

2.6.4. Overclock

There is an option to overclock the CPU of Raspberry Pi. Overclocking will add more power to our Raspberry Pi but it can reduce its life. When we click on this option we will get following warning:

```
Be aware that overclocking may reduce the lifetime
of your Raspberry Pi. If overclocking at a certain
level causes system instability, try a more modest
overclock. Hold down `shift` during boot to tempo-
rarily disable overclock.
```

2.6.5. Advanced options

• **SSH** – Here you can enable or disable remote command line access by SSH protocol. SSH is enabled by default and it allows us to access Raspberry Pi command line remotely.

• **Audio** – Here we can choose if we want audio sound to go through HDMI or 3.5 mm jack.

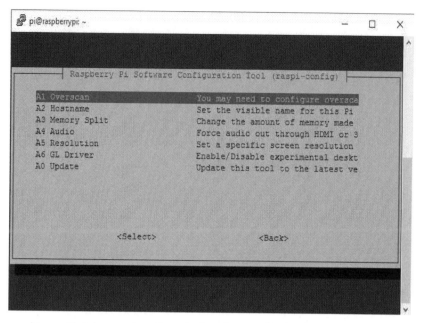

Image 7: Advanced options in Raspberry Pi`s Configuration tool

Chapter summary

In this chapter we learned how to set up Raspberry Pi. Whether you choose the usual way or through SSH protocol, they will have no influence on the further content that we are learning.

3.
Navigate Files, Folders, and Menus

3.1. File System Structure

Every operating system must have correct structure to function normally, and all applications, even the operating system have to respect it. For example, the programs should be allocated in a single folder, and configuration files in the configuration folder.

- /

  This is the root of the file system.
- /boot

  The boot directory contains information related to the booting process.
- /dev

  The dev directory contains device information such as hard drives.
- /sys

  The sys directory contains special files required by the operating systems.
- /proc

  The proc directory is a virtual directory containing a list of running processes.
- /etc

  Configuration files and located here along with user logins and encrypted passwords.
- /home

The home directory contains user data. When a user is created they will have a directory created here which will be the same as their user name. Default username is "pi", so it users directory would be "/home/pi".

- /root

  This is the home directory for the root user also known as super user. To set this up we need to use a Linux editor such as nano.
- /var

  This folder is used for files that change their size such as system and log files.
- /tmp

  This is the temporary directory.
- /sbin

- 'Executable files that are used for system maintenance are in this directory

- /bin

  Executable files exist here that are related to operating system files.
- /usr

  This contains programs that are used for user installed programs.
- /usr/local

  This contains files that have been installed locally.

3.2. Important files

To edit files from command line we need to use an Linux editor. There are few of them such as Nano, Vi, Emacs. We will use Nano editor, because it is easy to use and it is installed by default, so there is no need for additional installations. Simply type nano file.txt to edit file. Press CTRL+X to exit or CTRL+O to save file. We will access the important files by entering following commands:

- sudo nano /etc/wpa_supplicant/wpa_supplicant.conf

This file serves to adjust it for wireless connectivity to the Internet (Wi-Fi). You need to enter the SSID (name) of the network and password. In addition to these parameters, there are plenty of options that can be entered, for example, if the wireless network hidden. Once file is opened, go to the end of the file and add following code:

```
network={
    ssid="The_ESSID_from_earlier"
    psk="Your_wifi_password"
}
```

Change the default values to match your network parameters and restart Rasberry Pi with sudo reboot command. You can verify if Raspberry Pi was successfully connected to Wireless network by typing ifconfig wlan0 command. If filed inet addr has value, device was successfully connected. If not check your network parameters again.

- sudo nano /etc/default/keyboard

Entering this command we are opening Keyboard configuration file. This is usually necessary to change due to "#" difficulties. Raspberry Pi by default ships with GB keyboard layout. Pressing SHIFT + 3 we get "£" sign instead of "#".Fortunately, this can be solved quickly by changing keyboard layout from GB to US.

```
# KEYBOARD CONFIGURATION FILE

# Consult the keyboard(5) manual page.

XKBMODEL="pc105"
XKBLAYOUT="us"
XKBVARIANT=""
XKBOPTIONS=""


BACKSPACE="guess"
```

The parameters in this file indicate the following:

- XKBMODEL is the keyboard model variable
- XKBLAYOUT contains a list of layouts we want to use
- XKBVARIANT represents variable that store variants of the layout we intend to use
- XKBOPTIONS stores extra XKB configuration options such as shortcuts for swapping between keyboard layouts, such as grp:alt_shift_toggle (*SHIFT+ALT*)

3.3. Navigating menus in desktop environment

There are not many complicated menus on Raspbian operating system. There is one main menu you can reach by clicking on the raspberry, which is located in the top left corner. The main menu consists of several submenus such as programming, office, internet, games, accessories, help and preferences and shown on Image 8.

Image 8: Main menu on Raspbian operating system

Programming menu consists of many tools that we can use for development including Python 2 and 3 IDLE editor. In the office submenu LibreOffice tools are located and in the Internet submenu you can find different browsers. There are many games you can install on Raspberry Pi, however, not much hardware demanding. One of the usual games that comes preinstalled on this operating system is PI Minecraft Pi, Minecraft`s special version of game designed for this device. In the accessories you can find tools such as on-screen keyboard and similar. Help submenu offers Instruction manuals, guides and resources. In preferences we can find Raspberry Pi configuration. Configuration window offers us many things. From here we can changer Raspberry Pi`s name, choose boot preference (Desktop or Command Line), auto login, change password, enable SSH, etc.

Image 9: Raspberry Pi Configuration

4.

Write Python Programs Using the IDLE Editor

Let's start by downloading and installing. This program can be downloaded from the official website from the following link: *https://www.python.org/downloads/*. IDLE stands for Python's Integrated Development and Learning Environment. According to official documentation it has following features:

- coded in 100% pure Python, using the tkinter GUI toolkit

- cross-platform: works mostly the same on Windows, Unix, and Mac OS X

- Python shell window (interactive interpreter) with colorizing of code input, output, and error messages

- multi-window text editor with multiple undo, Python colorizing, smart indent, call tips, auto completion, and other features

- search within any window, replace within editor windows, and search through multiple files (grep)

- debugger with persistent breakpoints, stepping, and viewing of global and local namespaces

- configuration, browsers, and other dialogs

Once we land on download page, we can choose to download Python version 2 or 3. Difference between these two versions are small except that there is there is no more support and active development of Python version 2. Someone would use the version 2 only in the event that:

• The machine on which programming is carried out has installed Python version 2

• If we need specific third party package or utility that doesn't yet have released version that is compatible with Python 3.

Last stable Python version 2 is 2.7 while version 3 is 3.6 that came out in 2016. It is recommended for this tutorial to use Python 3 version.

After downloading and installing software, run it by finding it in your applications menu. On Image 10 we can see how Python IDLE editor looks like when it's opened.

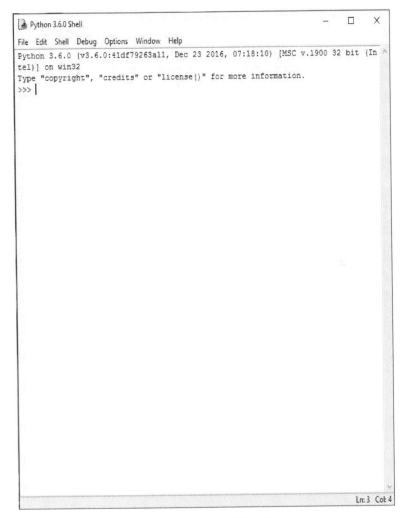

Image 10: Python IDLE editor

There are two ways to write programs in this editor:

• Write directly in the console

• Open a new document, write the entire program, save it, and then run it

In the text below we will show examples for both ways. Basically if a program is very small or we want to test something then we can write directly in the console, otherwise we should use second way.

4.1. Writing directly to console

When we write in the console we need to enter code row by row. After each row, we need to press enter to jump to the next one. For example:

```
print("Hello");
```

Output of this code will be just Hello as it can be seen on Image 11.

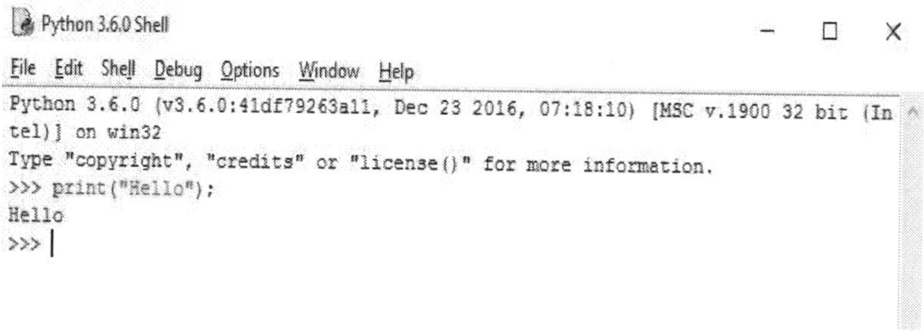

Image 11: Simple code to output string "Hello"

```
def printString(text):
        print(text);
        return
printString("Hello World");
```

When you type in the keyword "def", the program automatically recognizes that we want to write a function. After we entered the function, each click of ENTER button brings the typing console to the next line. We get out of the function by writing "return". After we are out of the function, we can simply call it passing string argument. When the above code is executed it will produce following result:

Hello World

On Image 12, we can see the above-mentioned process.

```
>>> def printString(text):
        print(text);
        return

>>> printString("Hello World");
Hello World
>>>
```

Image 12: Writing and executing function in the console of Python IDLE editor

More about the functions will be presented in the next chapter.

4.2. Writing to document

When we want to write Python program in this manner, it is necessary that in the editor we choose in the top left corner "File" option and then "New File" option. When we click on the "New File" option, new window will popup. First thing we need to do is to save file we want to work with. We can do that by clicking option "File" and then "Save", or simply by using command CTRL+S. After we saved our file, let's paste code from previous example into our new file. When our code is ready, we can run it simply by pressing option "Run" and then "Run Module" or F5 button. Note that if file is not saved it will prompt us to save it. On image 13 we can see how above-mentioned process looks like.

Image 13: Running Python file

Once we run it, it will be executed in main window or Python Shell as it is called. Image 14 show us how it looks when Python file is executed.

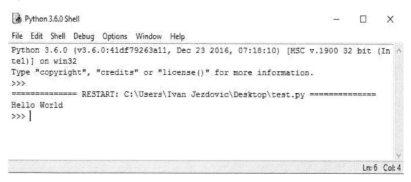

Image 14: Running program in Python Shell

4.3. Comments in Python

Comments in Python start with the hash character "#" and extend to the end of the line. Comments can appear at the beginning of the line, or after the code. They are mostly used to clarify code and they are not interpreted by Python. Let's show usage of Python comment on previous code:

```python
def printString(text): # defining new function
        print(text); # printing
        return
printString("Hello World"); #calling the func-
tion and passing argument
```

The above code will produce following output when executed:

```
Hello World
```

Basically adding comments didn't change our output, but it helps to clarify it.

Sometimes to explain something we will need more than one line. For that problem we can use multiline comments. Multiline comments start and end with triple quotes """ . In example bellow we will see how to use them.

```python
"""THIS IS MULTI
LINE COMMENT"""
def printString(text):
        print(text);
        return
printString("Hello World");
```

5.
Python Strings, Lists, Functions, and Dictionaries

5.1. Strings

String module contains a number of useful constants and classes as well as a large number of functions that are available as methods of the strings. Strings are one of the most popular data type in Python. They can be created by putting some characters between quotation marks. Python treats single quotes same as the double quotes. Creating string is simple as assigning value to a variable. For example:

```python
var1 = 'Hello World!'
var2 = "My name is Ivan."
```

5.1.1. Substrings

To access substring, we need to use square brackets. For example:

```python
#!/usr/bin/python

var1 = 'Hello World!'
var2 = "My name is Ivan."

print "var1[0]: ", var1[0]
print "var2[1:5]: ", var2[3:6]
```

We want to extract first letter from first string, and three letters from second string. Output from above code would be:

```
var1[0]:   H
var2[1:5]:   nam
```

5.1.2. Updating strings

To update string, all you need to do is to update variable that is holding the string we want to update with new value. That new value can be completely different or can be related with the previous one. For example:

```
#!/usr/bin/python

var1 = 'Hello World!'

print "Update", var1[:6] + 'Python'
```

When this code is executed, it produces following result:

```
Update: Hello Python
```

With the plus sign to the previous string we pasted the word "Python", but our new word started on the seventh position because of var1[:6] part of the code.

5.1.3. Escape characters

The "\" backslash character encodes difficult-to-type characters into a string. We use them if we want in the string to insert double quotes. For example:

```
''I don't ''know'' him.''
```

In this scenario Python will get confused because it will think the quotes around "know" represent end of the string. To solve this problem we are escaping double quotes.

"I don't \"know\" him."

There are many escape characters we might need. Below, in Table Three, you can find the most common escape characters and description for each one of them.

Backslash notation	Description
\a	Bell or alert
\b	Backspace
\cx	Control-x
\C-x	Control-x
\e	Escape
\f	Formfeed
\M-\C-x	Meta-Control-x
\n	Newline
\nnn	Octal notation, where n is in the range 0.7
\r	Carriage return
\s	Space

\t	Tab
\v	Vertical tab
\x	Character x
\xnn	Hexadecimal notation, where n is in the range 0.9, a.f, or A.F

Table 3: Escape characters

5.1.4. String operators

Table Four shows the special characters for string manipulation. In addition to the description of each character, there is a brief example. The values for the variables a and b are shown below.

Operator	Description	Example
+	Concatenation - Adds values on either side of the operator	a + b will give Hel-loWorld
*	Repetition - Creates new strings, concatenating multiple copies of the same string	a*2 will give - HelloHello
[]	Slice - Gives the character from the given index	a[1] will give e
[:]	Range Slice - Gives the characters	a[1:4] will

	from the given range	give ell
in	Membership - Returns true if a character exists in the given string	H in a will give 1
not in	Membership - Returns true if a character does not exist in the given string	M not in a will give 1
r/R	Raw String - Suppresses actual meaning of Escape characters. The syntax for raw strings is exactly the same as for normal strings with the exception of the raw string operator, the letter "r," which precedes the quotation marks. The "r" can be lowercase (r) or uppercase (R) and must be placed immediately preceding the first quote mark.	print r'\n' prints \n and print R'\n'prints \n
%	Format - Performs String formatting	

Table 4 String Special operators

5.1.5. Triple Quotes

Triple quotes are useful because they allow strings to span through multiple lines, including verbatim NEWLINEs, TABs and any other special characters. You can use three consecutive single or double quotes.

```
#!/usr/bin/python

para_str = """Raspberry Pi is a little credit
card-sized
computer that connects to your TV or monitor.
It is very powerful yet small device that allows
people of all ages to explore the  [ \n ] world
of computers
and learn how to program in languages
such as Python and Scratch."""
print para_str
```

When you perform the above written code, the result will be the following:

```
Raspberry Pi is a little credit card-sized
computer that connects to your TV or monitor.
It is very powerful yet small device that allows
people of all ages to explore the  [
 ] world of computers
and learn how to program in languages
such as Python and Scratch."""
```

5.1.6. Useful string methods

These methods are built-in and there is no need for additional installations.

- **capitalize()** - The first letter in a string is a uppercase.

- **find(str, beg=0 , end=len(string))**   - Determine if str occurs in string or in a substring of string if starting index beg and ending index end are given returns index if found and -1 otherwise.

• **index(str, beg=0, end=len(string))** - Same as find(), but raises an exception if str is not found.

• **isalnum()** - Returns true if string has at least 1 character and all characters are alphanumeric and false otherwise.

• **isalpha()** - Returns true if string has at least 1 character and all characters are alphabetic and false otherwise.

• **isdigit()** - Returns true if string contains only digits and false otherwise.

• **islower()** - Returns true if string has at least 1 cased character and all cased characters are in lowercase and false otherwise.

• **isnumeric()** - Returns true if a unicode string contains only numeric characters and false otherwise.

• **isupper()** - Returns true if string has at least one cased character and all cased characters are in uppercase and false otherwise.

• **len(string)** - Returns the length of the string

• **lower()** - Converts all uppercase letters in string to lowercase.

• **lstrip()** - Removes all leading whitespace in string.

• **split(str="", num=string.count(str))** - Splits string according to delimiter str (space if not provided) and returns list of substrings; split into at most num substrings if given.

• **startswith(str, beg=0,end=len(string))** - Determines if string or a substring of string (if starting index beg and ending index end are given) starts with substring str; returns true if so and false otherwise.

• **strip([chars])** - Performs both lstrip() and rstrip() on string

• **upper()** - Converts lowercase letters in string to uppercase.

• **isdecimal()** - Returns true if a unicode string contains only decimal characters and false otherwise.

5.2. Lists

Python lists can be written as a list of comma-separated values between square brackets. Entered values do not need to be of the same type. For example:

```
listOne= [2016, 2017, ``Raspberry'', ``Pi''];
listTwo = [1, ``a'', 2, ``b'', 3];
```

As with the strings, the first element is at the position 0.

5.2.1. Values in lists

To access an item in the list, we need to enter element position in square brackets next to a variable in which the list is located. In case we want to access more then one element, instead of element position we need to enter position interval. For example:

```
#!/usr/bin/python

listOne= [2016, 2017, ``Raspberry'', ``Pi''];
listTwo = [1, ``a'', 2, ``b'', 3];

print "listOne[0]: ", listOne [0]
```

When the above code is executed, it produces the following result:

```
listOne[0]: 2016
listTwo[2:4]: [2, "b", 3]
```

5.2.2. Updating lists

It is possible to update single or multiple elements of lists by entering element position you want to update in square brackets, next to variable that holds the list. For example:

```
#!/usr/bin/python

listOne= [2016, 2017, "Raspberry", "Pi"];

print listOne [2]
listOne[2] = 2018;
print listOne [2]
```

In code written above we change third element in the list from string "Raspberry" to integer value 2018. When we run the above written code, the result will be the next:

```
Raspberry
2018
```

5.2.3. Delete elements from list

To delete element from list, we can use del statement. For example:

```
#!/usr/bin/python

listOne = [2016, 2017, ``Raspberry'', ``Pi''];

print listOne
del listOne[2];
print listOne
```

With this code we want to delete third element of the list. When we run the code, we get following output:

```
[2016, 2017, ``Raspberry'', ``Pi'']
[2016, 2017, ``Pi'']
```

5.2.4. List operators

List operators are much like strings operators, and they even have the same behavior. In table five we will check out most common list operators.

Python Expression	Results	Description
len([2015, 2016, 2017])	3	Length
[1, 2, 3] + [4, 5, 6]	[1, 2, 3, 4, 5, 6]	Concatenation
[World!'] * 4	[World!', World!', World!', World!']	Repetition
3 in [1, 2, 3]	True	Membership
for x in [1, 2, 3]: print x,	1 2 3	Iteration

Table 5: List operators

5.2.5. List functions

Following functions are built-in and there is no need for additional installations.

- **cmp(list1, list2)** - Compares elements of both lists.
- **len(list)** - Gives the total length of the list.
- **max(list)** - Returns item from the list with max value.
- **min(list)** - Returns item from the list with min value.
- **list(seq)** - Converts a tuple into list.

5.2.6. List methods

Python includes following list methods:

• list.append(obj) - Appends object obj to list

• list.count(obj) - Returns count of how many times obj occurs in list

• list.extend(seq) - Appends the contents of seq to list

• list.index(obj) - Returns the lowest index in list that obj appears

• list.insert(index, obj) - Inserts object obj into list at offset index

• list.pop(obj=list[-1]) -Removes and returns last object or obj from list

• list.remove(obj) - Removes object obj from list

• list.reverse() - Reverses objects of list in place

• list.sort([func]) - Sorts objects of list, use compare func if given

An example of some of the above mentioned methods:

```
list = [1, 5, 3, 6, 9];
list;
list.insert(2, -1);
list;
list.sort();
list;
list.reverse();
list;
```

When we run above written code, we will get the following result:

```
list = [1, 5, 3, 6, 9];
list;
list.insert(2, -1);
list;
list.sort();
list;
list.reverse();
list;
```

5.3. Python functions

Functions allow us to order our code by dividing it into useful blocks. In this way, code is reusable and more readable. By using functions and reusing the code we can save some time. Defining the function is simple. Every function must begin with the reserved word "def". After "def" word we need to write the function name and the parenthesis. If we have any input parameters, they go inside the parenthesis. The code block within every function starts with a colon ":" and is indented. The return statement exits a function. It can pass expression back to the caller or if it doesn't have any arguments it returns "None". In example bellow we will see function that takes string as input parameter and prints it out.

```
def stringPrint(string):
        print(string);
        return
stringPrint("Hello World!");
```

Result:

```
Hello World!
```

After we defined function, we also called it and passed it input parameter. We call function simply by writing its name with parenthesis. If we have input parameter, we have to write it inside of parenthesis. It is very important to remember that if we define input parameter in function and call it without passing one, we will get an error.

5.3.1. Function arguments

There are few function arguments:

- **Required arguments**

  These arguments must be passed to a function in correct order. The number of arguments passed must match with function definition. An example of these arguments can be seen above.

- **Keyword arguments**

  If we use keyword arguments when calling a function, we do not take into account the order of parameters in function definition. By using keywords Python can match passed arguments with defined input parameters. For example:

```python
def stringPrint(str, year):
        print(str);
        print("Year: " , year);
        return
stringPrint(year=2017 str="Hello World!");
```

As we can see, when we defined function, first input parameter is "str" and second is "year". When we are calling function and passing arguments we are entering keywords .

Although the order is reversed, function will run smoothly and the result will be:

```
Hello World!
Year: 2017
```

• Default arguments

Default arguments are arguments that are taking default value that is defined inside the function if no other value is passed. Like in keyword arguments, order of parameters does not matter. In example bellow we will see how it works:

```
def printCar(car, year=2017):
        print("Vehicle: ", car,", Year: " ,
year);
        return
printCar(car="Mercedes Benz", year=2015);
printCar(car=``BMW'');
```

Output:

```
Vehicle:  Mercedes Benz , Year:  2015
Vehicle:  BMW , Year:  2017
```

First we call function with both parameters with keywords, and everything works as usual. Second time we passed only vehicle name and as we said above default argument was activated and we still got vehicle year, the default one (2017).

5.3.2. Changing input parameters inside function

Here is an example how we can change input parameter inside function.

```
def stringPrint(str):
        upper = str.upper();
        print(upper);
        return
stringPrint("Hello World!");
```

We entered as input parameter string "Hello World" with capital H and W, but inside function we called upper() string method and turned all the letters to uppercase. Output will be:

```
HELLO WORLD!
```

5.4. Python dictionaries

Dictionaries can be seen as some special lists and we can say that they behave the same as associative arrays in PHP. Each element in the dictionary consists of keys and values, and they are separated by a colon ":". Dictionaries begin and end with curly brackets. An empty dictionary looks like this: {}. Unlike the values, keys must be unique. Also, values can be of any type.

5.4.1. Creating dictionaries and accessing values

To access the value, it is necessary to enter the key in square brackets next to the variable in which dictionary is stored. For example:

```
#!/usr/bin/python

dictionary = {'Car': 'Mercedes', 'Year': 2017,
'Model': 'S Class'}

print "dictionary['Car']: ", dictionary['Car']
print "dictionary['Model']: ", diction-
ary['Model']
```

Output:

```
dictionary['Car']: Mercedes
dictionary['Model']: S Class
```

If we require information from the dictionary for a key that does not exist, we will get the following error.

```
#!/usr/bin/python

dictionary = {'Car': 'Mercedes', 'Year': 2017,
'Model': 'S Class'}

print "dictionary['Transmission']: ", diction-
ary['Transmission']
```

Following error:

```
dictionary['Transmission']:
Traceback (most recent call last):
    File "test.py", line 4, in <module>
        print "dictionary['Transmission']: ", dic-
tionary['Transmission'];
KeyError: 'Transmission'
```

5.4.2. Updating dictionaries

Similar to the lists, we execute this operation by selecting key and assigning a new value to it. For example:

```
#!/usr/bin/python

dictionary = {'Car': 'Mercedes', 'Year': 2017,
'Model': 'S Class'}

dictionary['Year'] = 2015; # update operation
dictionary['Transmission'] = "Manual"; # insert
operation


print "dictionary['Year']: ", dictionary['Year']
print "dictionary['Transmission']: ", diction-
ary['Transmission']
```

Output:

```
dictionary['Year']: 2015
dictionary['Transmission']: Manual
```

5.4.3. Delete elements from dictionary

We can delete items individually we can clear the entire dictionary or delete the whole dictionary. In the example below we will show all three options:

```python
#!/usr/bin/python

dictionary = {'Car': 'Mercedes', 'Year': 2017,
'Model': 'S Class'}

del dictionary['Car']; # remove data with key
''Car''
dictionary.clear();     # clear entire diction-
ary
del dictionary;        # delete entire dictionary

print "dictionary['Car']: ", dictionary['Car']
print "dictionary['Model']: ", diction-
ary['Model']
```

After executing this code we will get an error because after del dictionary, our dictionary does not exists any more and output will be following:

```
dictionary['Car']:
Traceback (most recent call last):
  File "test.py", line 8, in <module>
    print "dictionary['Car']: ", diction-
ary['Car'];
TypeError: 'type' object is unsubscriptable
```

When we talk about the dictionary keys it is very important to take into account following two things:

- The key must be unique. If in the dictionary two identical keys appear, key value is the one that was entered last.

- Keys must be immutable. A simple explanation of why the keys must be immutable is that if they are subject to change, it will no longer be possible to access their values.

5.4.4. Dictionary functions and methods

Functions and methods that follow are the ones that are used the most, and which are already built into the program so there is no need for additional installation.

- **cmp(dictionaryOne, dictionaryTwo2)** - Compares elements of both dictionaries.

- **len(dictionary)** - Gives the total length of the dictionary. Dictionary length represents number of elements in the dictionary.

- **str(dictionary)** - Produces a printable string representation of a dictionary

- **type(variable)** - Returns the type of the passed variable. If passed variable is dictionary, then it would return a dictionary type.

- **dictionary.clear()** - Removes all elements of dictionary

- **dictionary.copy()** - Returns a shallow copy of dictionary

- **dictionary.fromkeys()** - Create a new dictionary with keys from seq and values set to value.

- **dictionary.get(key, default=None)** - For key, returns value or default if key not in dictionary

- **dictionary.has_key(key)** - Returns true if key in dictionary, false otherwise

- **dictionary.items()** - Returns a list of dictionary`s (key, value) tuple pairs

- **dictionary.keys()** - Returns list of dictionary keys

- **dictionary.setdefault(key, default=None)** - Similar to get(), but will set dictionary[key]=default if key is not already in dict

- **dictionary.update(dictionaryTwo)** - Adds dictionary dictionaryTwo`s key-values pairs to dictionary

- **dictionary.values()** - Returns list of dictionary values

6.
GPIO Pins

Ability to interact with outside world comes from GPIO pins that are located on Raspberry Pi board. Since the GPIO pins are one of the most important parts of Raspberry Pi, for years they have been more and more improved. The latest Raspberry Pi 3 has 40 GPIO pins. Pins can be seen as switches that have two states, input and output. If we want to read data from sensors (i.e. temperature) we use input state, on the other hand if we want to turn on LED light we use output state.

Raspberry Pi 3 – GPIO Layout			
1.	3.3V	5V	2.
3.	GPIO2	5V	4.
5.	GPIO3	GND	6.
7.	GPIO4	GPIO14	8.
9.	GND	GPIO15	10.
11.	GPIO17	GPIO18	12.
13.	GPIO27	GND	14.
15.	GPIO22	GPIO23	16.
17.	3.3V	GPIO24	18.
19.	GPIO10	GND	20.
21.	GPIO9	GPIO25	22.
23.	GPIO11	GPIO8	24.
25.	GND	GPIO7	26.
27.	ID_SD	ID_SC	28.
29.	GPIO5	GND	30.
31.	GPIO6	GPIO12	32.
33.	GPIO13	GND	34.
35.	GPIO19	GPIO16	36.
37.	GPIO26	GPIO20	38.
39.	GND	GPIO21	40.

Table 6: Raspberry Pi 3 GPIO layout

In the table above we can see layout of GPIO pins on the Raspberry Pi 3 board. There are four colors, and therefore four types of pins. Red pins represent power, which have the strength of 3.3V or 5V. Black pins represent ground (output 0v and acts like the negative terminal of the battery). Yellow pins are GPIO pins that we can program. We have already mentioned that there are two states, input and output. When we use the output, pin can be set to HIGH (1) or LOW (0), depending on whether we want to turn on the power or not. When using input, in most cases, similar to the situation with the state of the output, we read 0 and 1 depending on the state of the sensor. We use orange pins if we want to connect additional boards.

6.1. Example – LED light

If we want to control LED light with Raspberry Pi 3 we need to do following:

1. Connect shorter wire of LED Light to appropriate resistor

2. Connect other side of resistor to GND pin on Raspberry Pi 3 Board

3. Connect longer wire of LED Light to any GPIO (Yellow) pin on Raspberry Pi 3 Board

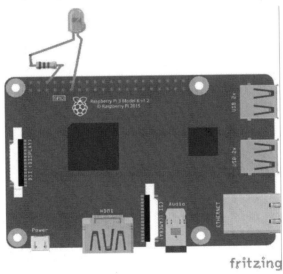

Image 15: LED Light connected to Raspberry Pi 3

In the example above, we use the GND pin and GPIO17 pin. By controlling GPIO17 pin, setting it to HIGH (1) or LOW (0), we control LED Light. After we have everything connected, we can quickly make a program in Python that will turn the light on or off. Advanced step would be to make web service. In that case, we could easily make web application or even android one to control lights in our home Later, in one of the next chapters we will extend this example and make a mini web application for managing it.

7.
Project ideas

We will start from the simple examples and go to the more complicated. Some of these examples will be presented in detail in the following chapters, and some of them will be left to you to implement them. Every idea will consist of a description and necessary equipment for its realization. In this chapter when we mention Raspberry Pi device as a component, we mean all associated components such as Ethernet cable, charger and so on.

7.1. LED light

As we can see in the previous chapter, this is one of the simplest examples for Raspberry Pi and it also requires minimum additional components. Idea here is to operate LED light from web application. It should be simple app with two buttons, switch on and switch off. To complete this project, it is necessary to have the following components:

- Raspberry Pi with all necessary equipment
- 1 LED light
- 1 resistor depending on power of LED light

More about resistors, as well as the colors on them can be found at the following link
http://www.digikey.com/en/resources/conversion-calculators/conversion-calculator-resistor-color-code-4-band.

7.2. Streaming music

Let your Raspberry Pi device becomes fun for the whole crew. Raspberry Pi should be connected to the home network, but also with stereo speakers (or any speakers that have a 3.5mm output). After preparing and installing the required programs on the Raspberry Pi device, each household that is connected to the local network will be able to wirelessly select and play music via smart phone or computer. Raspberry Pi can read the local music from your smartphone music from a pre-made media server. There are many tutorials on the Internet that explain how this can be implemented. There are also special applications for your smartphone that works via UPnP (Universal Plug and Play) protocol like BubbleUPnP. To complete this project, it is necessary to have the following components:

- Raspberry Pi with all necessary equipment
- 3.5mm speakers
- Smart phone

7.3. Smart fire alarm

This is simply example of connecting sensor to Raspberry Pi, in this case sensor for flame detection. The sensor for flame detection should be place somewhere high and fixed to the wall. Also it should have 2 LED light that indicates its status. We should use green LED light for normal activity and red LED light if flame is spotted. The device should have a warning system and there are few ways to implement it. The most important alert must be on site, near Raspberry Pi, and the best way to do it is by connecting a buzzer. As for the wireless warning, we can choose several ways, such as warning via SMS, web applications or mobile applications. To complete this project, it is necessary to have the following components:

- Raspberry Pi with all necessary equipment
- 1 green LED light
- 1 red LED light
- Flame detector
- Cables

7.4. Smart city – Measuring temperature and humidity

Sensor DHT11 for measuring temperature and humidity could be found integrated into street lamps. In the immediate vicinity of the sensor Wi-Fi module should be located as well as the Raspberry Pi micro-computer. Street lamps should contain power for Raspberry Pi and all necessary equipment. The sensor should perform readings of temperature and humidity, and to store data in the database. The user will have access to the web application where he could see the current temperature and humidity, but also to obtain an advice on how to dress in accordance with the current weather conditions. To complete this project, it is necessary to have the following components:

- Raspberry Pi with all necessary equipment
- DHT 11 sensor for temperature and humidity measuring
- 10000Ω resistor
- Smart phone

7.5. Smart garbage disposal

Smart control of disposal using motion sensors should allow detecting the presence of people close to the container, and an ultrasonic sensor should detect level of waste in the container. When the man approaches, the container is automatically opened by the actuator, and waste can be disposed. For the realization of this project we need 2 sensors, actuator (motor), LEDs, as well as web applications that shows the capacity of the container. Actuator is placed on the lid of the container and represents a mechanism that handles opening and closing of the container. Motion sensor is located on the container and performs the detection of the presence of the citizens. The ultrasonic sensor is located in a container, and rather precisely measures the distance from the bottom to the top of the container. Ultrasonic sensor constantly measures the amount of waste that is in container and prints the information on the web application. At each waste disposal, a citizen would receive a notification via SMS that there was a garbage disposal. If container capacity exceeds 90% red LED will be activated and notification will be sent to the competent service through SMS that says that container is full and must be emptied.

7.6. Smart aquarium

Smart aquarium should enable user to feed the fishes with the application, send a notice of the level of water in the tank and the amount of temperature and humidity. Realization of this project requires 2 sensors (ultrasonic sensor for water level and sensor for temperature and humidity), the motor to start the feeders, and responsive web applications. The ultrasonic sensor is used for measuring the water level in the tank. On command, the user initiates a motor, a motor drives feeder. All measured data at any time is available to user and can be seen through web application.

7.7. Smart agriculture

Smart Agriculture should provide automated watering of large areas like fields, football pitches. It should also send notification of the water flow and soil moisture, as well as information about the time of each watering. All information should be displayed in the web application. For the realization, this project requires 2 sensors, solenoid valve, relay and web application. Soil moisture sensor should be stabbed in the soil that needs to be watered. Once the soil moisture drops below normal state, relay should be activated and let current to the electromagnetic valve. Once electromagnetic valve gets current it starts watering the land. Based on the sensor for water flow, we will measure the amount of water needed for irrigation and the data will be displayed on a web application. Also based on the water flow, we could calculate our costs for a given accounting period.   During each watering of the desired surface, the information will be displayed on the web application. The advantage of this model is that the solenoid valve is attached directly to the water supply, which means that our surface irrigation will never be left without the required amount of water. After watering, the soil moisture sensor will detect that achieved normal soil moisture and then turn off the relay that will stop the operation of a solenoid valve.   To complete this project, it is necessary to have the following components:

- Raspberry Pi with all necessary equipment
- Water flow sensor
- Solenoid valve
- Soil moisture sensor
- Relay
- Cables
- Hoses

8.
Accessories for the Raspberry Pi

There are many accessories for Raspberry Pi and in this chapter we will list some of them and describe them in detail. With the advent of Raspberry Pi 3, demand for accessories such as Wi-Fi and Bluetooth adapters significantly decreased. In addition to the one-piece accessories, there are accessories kits, few of them we will mention in the text bellow.

8.1. Breadboard

It represents an essential component of any project. It is a very useful device for prototyping circuits. Using this component, we can easily plug in or out various sensors or actuators without the need for soldering. A breadboard has many holes, spaced by 0.1 inch. There are many variations of breadboard. Some of them have one section, but usually they are made with two sections. Those with two sections have a small bridge in the center that runs from one side to another and it divides one section from another. Also on each section there are two long rows that are designed to provide easy access to ground and power. They are called power rails.

8.2. Raspberry Pi Heat Sink

Attaching Heat Sinks to Raspberry Pi helps to keep it cool and prevents overheating. They usually come with adhesive thermal layer and they are made from aluminum. It also reduces the risk of hardware failure. Heat sinks are small and fit with all Raspberry cases. They come in different sizes for different components we want to cool down, such as CPU or GPU.

8.3. Raspberry Pi Camera module

There are two version of Raspberry Pi Camera, and the latest is v2. It can be used to take HD video as well as photographs. It is very easy for beginners used, but also provides a lot of possibilities for experienced developers. In contrast to first version of the camera that had a 5 megapixel lens, the version 2 is improved and it has 8 megapixels. It supports 1080p30, 720p60 and VGA90 video modes. Camera comes with 15cm cable. On the official website they advise that the cable length should not change, because it affects the quality of the camera. However, enthusiasts who like to work with Raspberry Pi camera did a HDMI adapter. With the help of this adapter, we can use HDMI cable to extend the distance between device and camera.

8.4. Raspberry Pi Case

The box for the device is very important if it is being transported. On the one hand, there are advantages such as protection, and on the other there are also disadvantages such as lack of access to the pins and the device with a case takes up more space. There is an official case for the Raspberry Pi device, but you can also find a lot non-original cases. Even you can make yourself a case, but you need to pay attention to the cooling and the openings for cables. According to the official Raspberry Pi website their case has following features:

- High-quality ABS construction
- Removable side panels and lid for easy access to GPIO, camera and display connectors
- Light pipes for power and activity LEDs
- Extraordinarily handsome

8.5. Raspberry Pi displays

There are many different types of displays for Raspberry Pi such as monochrome LCD displays, with one or more lines, a small touch screens and large touch screens of 7 inches or more. Touch screens give us ability to turn Raspberry Pi to all-in-one device. Raspberry Pi`s official 7 inch touch screen has 800 x 480 display resolution and it connects to the Raspberry Pi via an adapter board which handles power and signal conversion. Only two connections to the Pi are required, power from the GPIO port and ribbon cable that connects to the DSI port. Touchscreen supports up to 10 finger touch.

8.6. Raspberry Pi Canakit

The kit comes with many components. It comes in plain white cardboard box filled with all equipment. It contains Raspberry Pi 3 and black plastic case for it. It also contains:

- 2.5A power supply
- 150mbps 802.11 USB Wi-Fi adapter
- HDMI cable
- 32GB Micro SD card (Class 10)
- Heat sink
- GPIO and Resistor Colors Quick Reference Cards
- CanaKit GPIO to Breadboard Interface Board
- GPIO Ribbon Cable
- Full-Size Large Breadboard
- 32 x M/M Jumper Wires
- 10 x M/F Jumper Wires
- RGB LED

- 2 x Red LEDs

- 2 x Green LEDs

- 2 x Yellow LEDs

- 2 x Blue LEDs

- 2 x Push Button Switches

- 10 x 220 Ohm Resistors

- 5 x 10K Ohm Resistors

- CanaKit General Guide for Beginners to Electronic Components

- CanaKit General Assembly Guide

This kit is one of the most popular on the market and it also comes with 1-Year Manufacturer Warranty.

9.
Tips and Tricks

For each device and operating system, there are certain rules and guidelines by which to we comply with while using them. However, there are shortcuts that make our everyday use easier. Some of them will be shown below, and some of them you will find by yourself while using the device.

9.1. Download Chromium

If you want to surf the web, you'll come up on sites with lots of JavaScript and loading speed will be very slow. A decent alternative to Epiphany and Iceweasel when it comes to handling such sites and services is Chromium - the open-source browser that Chrome is based on.

9.2. Use a script blocker

Another way to bypass the lag and hiccups when surfing on the web is to completely exclude loading of the scripts. This can be done by installing Mozilla's browser for Linux called Iceweasel. After installing Iceweasel we need to go to Mozilla`s add-on page and install NoScript extension. This extension will block JavaScript across web, which will increase the speed at which pages load. Of course, there is a drawback to using this script, and that is that some, perhaps essential, part of the content will not be displayed. Certainly, in the upper right corner there is an icon of this extension where we can choose which script we want to be loaded afterwards.

9.3. Do not attempt to run more things at once

This device has only 1GB of RAM, so its potential for multitasking is limited. Try to avoid opening two browsers in same time or more than four tabs in one. Also try to avoid opening browser and heavy programs like LibreOffice or similar, because Raspberry Pi could get stuck.

9.4. FING - replacement for Advanced IP Scanner

Fing is a mobile application that allows you to scan a network and is available for both Android and iOS platform. It is super-fast and very easy to use. Besides that it also allows you to scan ports, lookup DNS and ping devices. It also has option to create your profile where you can store, backup and identify devices.

9.5. HDMI to VGA adapter

In case you do not have a monitor or TV with the HDMI output, you can use HDMI to VGA adapter. This device is very small and very cheap and with it you can easily connect an old monitor with Raspberry Pi. Pay attention when purchasing this device, because some versions do not support audio. It is important to know that adapter operates only from HDMI source to VGA, it is not bi-directional. Usually it supports video resolution up to 1080p.

10.

Advanced Circuits and Examples with the Raspberry Pi 3

In this chapter we will explain in detail and show some of the above-mentioned project ideas. We will start from easier to more difficult projects. In every a bit of knowledge of web technologies will be necessary. Each project idea explained in this chapter will consist of several parts:

- Detailed table with the necessary devices
- Wiring diagram drawn in Fritzing
- Python code for Raspberry Pi
- All necessary codes for web application
- Screenshots of finished project

10.1. LED Light

10.1.1. Detailed table with the necessary devices

Name	Image	Comment	Quantity
Raspberry Pi 3		Single board computer	1
Smartphone		Any smart phone that is able to access the web application	1

Ethernet cable		Cable longer than 1m is recommended for ease of moving the device	1
LED Light		Any size	1
Resistor		Depending on LED type y	1
Mouse		Requires mouse with USB connection	1
Keyboad		Requires keyboard with USB connection	1
Breadboard		To connect electronic components without soldering	1
Cables		Male-Female	2

MicroUSB charger		If you connect devices that require more power, such as internet modem, it is necessary to use a stronger charger, at least 2A	1
HDMI kabl		Cable longer than 1m is recommended for ease of moving the device	1
Monitor		Support for HDMI is required	1

Table 7: Components needed for LED Light project

10.1.2. Wiring diagram drawn in Fritzing

The image below contains LED light, resistor and Raspberry Pi. You could connect LED Light directly to Raspberry Pi or use breadboard and cable while practicing. One side of resistor is connected to shorter leg od LED light (negative) and the other side is connected to Raspberry Pi Ground pin (GND). Longer leg of LED light is connected to GPIO17 pin. We will use this pin to control light.

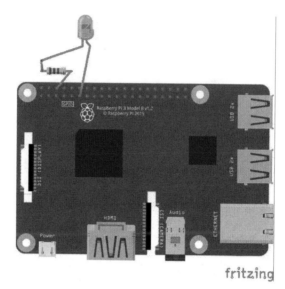

Image 16 Wiring diagram for LED Light project

10.1.3. Python code for Raspberry Pi

The script below is Python webserver, made with the help of web.py library. To install web.py library all we need to do is run following line of code:

```
pip install web.py
```

After running this line of code, we can use it later in our server script.

```
#importing libraries
import web
import RPi.GPIO as GPIO
import json

# defining paths
urls = (
```

```python
    '/', 'index',
    '/turnon', 'turnOn',
    '/turnoff', 'turnOff'


)


GPIO.setmode(GPIO.BCM)
GPIO.setup(17, GPIO.OUT)



# Functions that are executed for each path.

class index:
    def GET(self):
        page = open("page.html", "r").read()
        return page
class turnOn:
    def GET(self):
        GPIO.output(17, GPIO.HIGH)
        data={}
        data["msg"]="LED ON!"
        return json.dumps(data)
class turnOff:
    def GET(self):
        GPIO.output(17, GPIO.LOW)
        data={}
        data["msg"]="LED OFF!"
        return json.dumps(data)


#starting the server
if __name__ == "__main__":
```

```
app = web.application(urls, globals())
app.run()
```

After finishing of typing the code, the file should be saved under the name server.py. Location to save the file on your computer can be any. In this case, the script is saved on the Desktop. If we are in the /home/pi folder, to start the script that is on the desktop, we need to enter the following two commands:

```
cd Desktop
sudo python server.py
```

After running these two commands Python program will start webserver. Ending the execution of program is done with Ctrl+C command.

10.1.4. All necessary codes for Web application

```html
<!DOCTYPE html>
<html>
<head>
        <title>LED Light</title>
        <script
src="https://ajax.googleapis.com/ajax/libs/jquer
y/2.2.4/jquery.min.js"></script>

        <!-- Latest compiled and minified CSS -->
        <link rel="stylesheet"
href="https://maxcdn.bootstrapcdn.com/bootstrap/
3.3.7/css/bootstrap.min.css" integrity="sha384-
BVYiiSIF-
eK1dGmJRAkycuHAHRg32OmUcww7on3RYdg4Va+PmSTsz/K68
vbdEjh4u" crossorigin="anonymous">

        <!-- Latest compiled and minified JavaS-
cript -->
        <script
src="https://maxcdn.bootstrapcdn.com/bootstrap/3
.3.7/js/bootstrap.min.js" integrity="sha384-
Tc5IQib027qvyjSMfHjOMaLkfuWVxZxUPnCJA712mCWNIpG9
mGCD8wGNIcPD7Txa" cros-
sorigin="anonymous"></script>
        <style>
                body {
                        margin-top: 10px;
                }
        </style>
```

```
    <script>
            function turnOn () {
                    $.getJSON(
"http://192.168.0.18:8080/turnon", function( da-
ta ) {

                            alert(data.msg);
                    });
            }
            function turnOff () {
                    $.getJSON(
"http://192.168.0.18:8080/turnoff", function(
data ) {

                            alert(data.msg);
                    });
            }

    </script>
</head>
<body>
    <div class="container">
            <div class="col-lg-4"></div>
            <div class="col-lg-4">
                    <div class="alert alert-
info text-center">LED Light</div>
                    <div class="well">
                            <button on-
click="turnOn();" class="btn btn-success btn-
block">Turn On</button>
                            <button on-
click="turnOff();"  class="btn btn-danger btn-
block">Turn Off</button>
                    </div>
            </div>
            <div class="col-lg-4"></div>
```

```
        </div>
    </body>
</html>
```

After finishing of typing the code, the file should be saved under the name page.html and stored on Raspberry Pi desktop. Web application can be accessed by entering the IP address of Raspberry Pi devices and port 8080. Port 8080 is default web.py port. Web application is pretty simple. We are having two buttons with "onclick" events that are triggering two JavaScript functions. Each function is calling Python`s webserver path and alerts returned data to user.

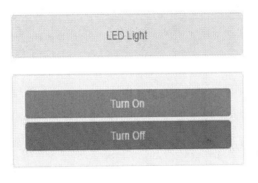

Image 17: LED Light Web application

10.2. Smart city – Measuring temperature and humidity

10.2.1. Detailed table with the necessary devices

All components necessary for the development of this project are given in Table 5

Name	Image	Comment	Quantity
Raspberry Pi 3		Single board computer	1
Temperature and humidity sensor		DHT11	1
Smartphone		Any smart phone that is able to access the web application	1
Ethernet cable		Cable longer than 1m is recommended for ease of moving the device	1

Resistor		10000Ω	1
Mouse		Requires mouse with USB connection	1
Keyboad		Requires keyboard with USB connection	1
Breadboard		To connect electronic components without soldering	1
Cables		Male-male	4
Cables		Male-Female	3
MicroUSB charger		If you connect devices that require more power, such as internet modem, it is necessary to	1

		use a stronger charger, at least 2A	
HDMI kabl		Cable longer than 1m is recommended for ease of moving the device	1
Monitor		Support for HDMI is required	1

Table 8: Components for needed for Smart City project

10.2.2. Wiring diagram drawn in Fritzing

The image below shows the DHT11 sensor that measures temperature and humidity. The sensor contains 4 pins, of which only 3 are used in our project. When the sensor is facing towards the user, starting from the left, the first pin represents POWER, the second is a digital output pin, the third pin is an analog pin (which we do not use) and fourth pin represents GROUND.

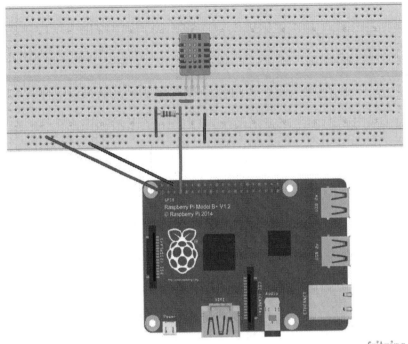

fritzing

Image 18: Wiring diagram for Smart City project

The black lines in the image represent the cables that connect to the ground (negative) on the Raspberry Pi device. Red lines in the image represent the cables that connect to 3.3 V power to Raspberry Pi device. Purple lines represent connections to components on breadboard with appropriate GPIO pins on the Raspberry Pi device.

10.2.3. Python code for Raspberry Pi

Before we run down written code, we need to install AdaFruit module on our device. The process is very easy and includes several steps. We must first download the module from the Internet. Let's position ourselves in /home/pi directory and execute following lines:

```
git clone
https://github.com/adafruit/Adafruit_Python_DHT.
git
cd Adafruit_Python_DHT
```

First line downloads the module, and with second line we are entering into Adafruit folder that we just downloaded. Before installing module we need to install few dependencies. We can do that with following lines of code:

```
sudo apt-get update
sudo apt-get install build-essential python-dev
python-openssl
```

If you see an error that a package is already installed or at the latest version, don't worry you can ignore it and move on. Next part is to install the library execute with command:

```
sudo python setup.py install
```

This should compile the code for the library and install it on your device so we can access AdaFruit DHT module from our Python script.

```
#!/usr/bin/python
import time #importing time library
import urllib #library for external url usage
import Adafruit_DHT as dht #library for DHT11
sensor
while True:
        h,t = dht.read_retry(dht.DHT11,4)
#reading temperature and humidity
        print 'Temp = {0:0.1f}*C
Humidity={1:0.1f}%'.format(t,h) #printing data
        url=
'http://www.example.com/writeData.php?temp={0}&h
```

```
umi={1}'.format(t,h) #calling a webservice that
inserts data to database
        urllib.urlopen(url) #execution of the
above request
        time.sleep(3) # measurement of
temperature and humidity every 3 seconds
```

After finishing of typing the code, the file should be saved under the name temphumi.py. Location to save the file on your computer can be any. In this case, the script is saved on the Desktop. If we are in the /home/pi folder, to start the script that is on the desktop, we need to enter the following two commands:

```
cd Desktop
sudo python temphumi.py
```

After running these two commands Python program will start measuring temperature and humidity and send it to web service as well. Ending the execution of program is done with Ctrl+C command.

10.2.4. All necessary codes for web application

To realize this project we need to build small web service and database. There are many free hosting places where you can create a database and set up scripts that follow below or you can do it all locally.

First this we should do is to make database and connect to it. We will use MySQL database named "rpi". Database will have one table named "temphumi" and four columns "temphumiid", "temp"," humi" and "time". Column types can be seen on image bellow.

#	Name	Type	Collation	Attributes	Null	Default	Extra
1	temphumiid	int(11)			No	None	AUTO_INCREMENT
2	temp	double			No	None	
3	humi	double			No	None	
4	time	datetime			No	None	

Image 19: Database layout for Smart City project

The script that follows enables us to connect to the database.Note that you need to enter your username and password.

```php
<?php
$db_server = "localhost";
$db_db= "rpi";
$db_user = "root";
$db_pass = "";
$mysqli = new mysqli($db_server, $db_user,
$db_pass, $db_db);
if ($mysqli->connect_errno) {
    printf("Connection error: %s\n", $mysqli-
>connect_error);
    exit();
}
$mysqli->set_charset("utf8");
?>
```

After finishing of typing the code, the file should be saved under the name connection.php and stored on webserver.

Next script takes data sent from Raspberry Pi and inserts it into the database.

```php
<?php
        include 'konekcija.php';

        $temp = $_GET['temp']; //getting
temperature
        $humi = $_GET['humi'];//getting humidity
        $sql="INSERT INTO temphumi (temp, humi,
vreme) VALUES ('".$temp."', '".$humi."',
NOW())"; //inserting data to database
        $q=$mysqli->query($sql); //executing
query

    ?>
```

After finishing of typing the code, the file should be saved under the name writeData.php and stored on webserver.

The script that follows takes the data from the database, processes it and returns it in a format suitable for reading by a web application.

```php
<?php
header("Content-type: application/json");
require "connection.php";

 //colon preparation for google chart
visualization

    $array['cols'][] = array('label' => Time,
'type' => 'string');
```

```php
    $array['cols'][] = array('label' =>
Temperature (*C)', 'type' => 'number');
    $array['cols'][] = array('label' => Humidity
(%)', 'type' => 'number');


// Reading from the database and storing data in
the array

$sql="SELECT * FROM temphumi";
if (!$q=$mysqli->query($sql)){
// if the query does not execute
echo '{"error":"Error while executing query."}';
exit();
} else {
//if query is executed
if ($q->num_rows>0){
//if there are results in database
$niz = array();
while ($row=$q->fetch_object()){

        $array['rows'][] = array('c' => array(
array('v'=>$row->time),array('v'=>$row-
>temp),array('v'=>$row->humi)) );


}

//creating json

$niz_json = json_encode ($array);

print ($niz_json);
} else {
//if there are no results in database
echo '{"error":"Error - No results."}';
```

```
}
}?>
<?php
$mysqli->close();

?>
```

After finishing of typing the code, the file should be saved under the name readData.php and stored on webserver.

Code that follows show us how web application is made. For the design we are using Bootstrap. Beside that we are using JavaScript and PHP to handle some logic operations and reading from database. To draw a graph we are using Google's service Google Charts. You can read more about Google Charts   by   visiting   following   link *https://developers.google.com/chart/*.

```
<!DOCTYPE html>
<html>
  <head>
    <title>Smart City</title>
    <style type="text/css">
    #temp {
      text-align: center;
      margin: 5px;
    }

    </style>
    <?php include "connection.php"; ?>
```

```
    <link rel="stylesheet"
href="https://maxcdn.bootstrapcdn.com/bootstrap/
3.3.7/css/bootstrap.min.css" integrity="sha384-
BVYiiSIF-
eK1dGmJRAkycuHAHRg32OmUcww7on3RYdg4Va+PmSTsz/K68
vbdEjh4u" crossorigin="anonymous">
    <meta http-equiv='Content-Type' con-
tent='Type=text/html; charset=utf-8'>
    <!--Loading Google Chart API-->
    <script type="text/javascript"
src="https://www.google.com/jsapi"></script>
    <!--Loading jQuery-->
    <script
src="https://ajax.googleapis.com/ajax/libs/jquer
y/2.1.3/jquery.min.js"></script>
    <script type="text/javascript">
    // Loading visualization API
    google.load('visualization', '1', {'packag-
es':['corechart']});
    // Sends callback when API is loaded
    google.setOnLoadCallback(drawGraph);
    function drawGraph() {
      var jsonData = $.ajax({
      url:
"http://www.example.com/readData.php",
      dataType:"json",
      async: false
    }).responseText;
    // It creates a table with data based on
JSON
    var data = new
google.visualization.DataTable(jsonData);
    //data.setColumns([0,1]);
    var options = {'title':Temperature,
```

```
        'height':400};

    // Instantiates a chart
    var chart = new
google.visualization.LineChart(document.getEleme
ntById('chart_div'));



    chart.draw(data,  options);


  }
  </script>
  </head>
<body>
  <div class="row" id="temp">

<div class="col-lg-6" >
<h2> Current temperature</h2>
<div id="temprefresh">
<?php
$sql="SELECT * FROM temphumi ORDER BY temphumiid
DESC";
$q=$mysqli->query($sql);
$row=$q->fetch_object();



  ?>
  <div class="alert alert-info"> Current tempera-
ture: <?php echo $row->temp; ?> *C</div>
  <div class="alert alert-success"> <?php
```

```
if ($row->temp ==null){
 echo " I'm waiting for the temperature!";
  } else {
 if ($row->temp >=27) echo " Put on a shirt.";
?>
 <?php if ($row->temp >=20 && $row->temp <=26)
echo " Put on a sweatshirt."; ?>
 <?php if ($row->temp <=19) echo " Put on a
jacket.";
 }
 ?></div>
</div>
</div>

<div class="col-lg-6">
  <h2>Graph</h2>
<div id="chart_div"></div>

</div>

</div>
<script
src="https://maxcdn.bootstrapcdn.com/bootstrap/3
.3.7/js/bootstrap.min.js" integrity="sha384-
Tc5IQib027qvyjSMfHjOMaLkfuWVxZxUPnCJA712mCWNIpG9
mGCD8wGNIcPD7Txa" cros-
sorigin="anonymous"></script>
</body>
</html>
```

Web application prints the current temperature along with advice on how to properly wear, and in addition it provides a graphical display of temperature and humidity.

10.3. Smart agriculture

10.3.1. Detailed table with the necessary devices

All components necessary for the development of this project are given in Table 5

Name	Image	Comment	Quantity
Raspberry Pi 3		Single board computer	1
Ethernet cable		Cable longer than 1m is recommended for ease of moving the device	1
Water flow sensor		YF-S201	1
Soil moisture sensor		With LM393 comparator circuit	1

Water hose		Okiten 3/4 " pressure up to 10 bars	
Solenoid valve		KHAN AC-220V	1
Relay		5V DC	1
Mouse		Requires mouse with USB connection	1
Keyboad		Requires keyboard with USB connection	1
Cables		Male-male	2
Cables		Male-Female	5

MicroUSB charger		If you connect devices that require more power, such as internet modem, it is necessary to use a stronger charger, at least 2A	1
HDMI kabl		Cable longer than 1m is recommended for ease of moving the device	1
Monitor		Support for HDMI is required	1

Table 9: Components needed for Smart agriculture project

10.3.2. Wiring diagram drawn in Fritzing

The black lines on the image represent the cables that are to the ground (negative) on the Raspberry Pi device. Red lines on the image represent the cables that connect to power (3.3V and 5.0V) from the Raspberry Pi device. Yellow lines represent the connection of the components with the appropriate GPIO pins on the Raspberry Pi device. Green lines represent connecting electromagnetic valve with a voltage of 220V and a link between analogue sensor that measures soil moisture and its digital controller.

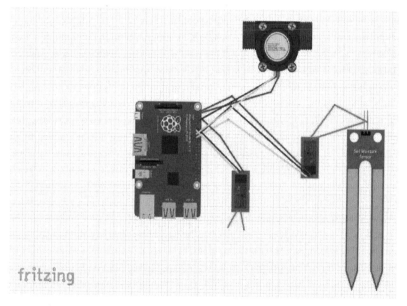

Image 20: Wiring diagram for Smart agriculture project

It is important to note that the solenoid valve is not directly connected to Raspberry Pi device, but it is managed through a relay. That is why it is not on the wiring diagram.

10.3.3. Python code for Raspberry Pi

Given that this is a little more complicated project, we will have more python scripts. Also, Raspberry Pi device will serve us as a web server. Web server will be made in Python using web.py library. In addition, we will work a bit with threads. The first two Python scripts apply only to turning on and off the relay.

```python
#!/usr/bin/python

#Importing required libraries
import RPi.GPIO as GPIO
import time

# Using BCM system
GPIO.setmode(GPIO.BCM)

# List of pins that are used
pinList = [17]

# seting the pins to HIGH

for i in pinList:
    GPIO.setwarnings(False)
    GPIO.setup(i, GPIO.OUT)
    GPIO.output(i, GPIO.HIGH)

def trigger() :
        for i in pinList:
            GPIO.output(i, GPIO.HIGH)
#            GPIO.cleanup()
```

```
        break


try:
    trigger()


except KeyboardInterrupt:
  print "  Quit"
  # Reseting GPIO settings
  GPIO.cleanup()
```

After finishing of typing the code, the file should be saved under the name **relayon.py**. Location to save the file on your computer can be any. In this case, the script is saved on the Desktop.

```
#!/usr/bin/python

# Importing required libraries
import RPi.GPIO as GPIO
import time

# Using BCM system
GPIO.setmode(GPIO.BCM)

# List of pins that are used

pinList = [17]

# seting the pins to LOW

for i in pinList:
    GPIO.setwarnings(False)
```

```
    GPIO.setup(i, GPIO.OUT)
    GPIO.output(i, GPIO.HIGH)


def trigger() :
        for i in pinList:
            GPIO.output(i, GPIO.LOW)
#           GPIO.cleanup()
            break



try:
    trigger()



except KeyboardInterrupt:
    print "  Quit"
    # Reseting GPIO settings
    GPIO.cleanup()
```

After finishing of typing the code, the file should be saved under the name **relayoff**.py. Location to save the file on your computer can be any. In this case, the script is saved on the Desktop.

Code that follows automatically checks the soil moisture and if necessery starts watering.

```
# Importing required libraries

import RPi.GPIO as GPIO
import time, sys
import os

GPIO.setmode(GPIO.BCM)
```

```
GPIO.setup(22, GPIO.IN)

while True:
        state = GPIO.input(22)
        if state==1:
                os.system("sudo python
relejon.py")
                time.sleep(5)
                os.system("sudo python
relejoff.py")
                time.sleep(10)
```

After finishing of typing the code, the file should be saved under the name **soilmoisture.py**. Location to save the file on your computer can be any. In this case, the script is saved on the Desktop.

Script that follows measures water flow and starts or stops watering.

```
#!/usr/bin/env python

import RPi.GPIO as GPIO
import time, sys
import os
import urllib

FLOW_SENSOR = 27

GPIO.setmode(GPIO.BCM)


global count
count = 0
```

```
def pulseEvent(liter):
        GPIO.cleanup()
        GPIO.setmode(GPIO.BCM)
        GPIO.setup(FLOW_SENSOR, GPIO.IN,
pull_up_down = GPIO.PUD_UP)
        def countPulse(channel):
                liter2 = float(liter)
                global count
                count = count+1
                digit =
round((count/float(450)),2)
                print digit
                if (digit >= liter2):
                        count=0

        url="http://localhost:8080/turnoff"
                urllib.urlopen(url)
                global pumpstatus
                pumpstatus=0
                sys.exit("Done")
            else:
                print "Error"
            print "Flow: %s l" % digit
        GPIO.add_event_detect(FLOW_SENSOR,
GPIO.FALLING, callback=countPulse)
```

After finishing of typing the code, the file should be saved under the name **waterflow.py**. Location to save the file on your computer can be any. In this case, the script is saved on the Desktop.

The script below is Python webserver, made with the help of web.py library. To install web.py library all we need to do is run following line of code:

```
pip install web.py
```

After running this line of code, we can use it later in our server script.

```
#importing libraries
import web
import os
import webbrowser
from waterflow import pulseEvent
import json

# definingpaths
urls = (
    '/', 'index',
    '/turnon', 'pumpOn',
    '/turnoff', 'pumpOff',
    '/turnLiter', 'turnLiter',
    '/pumpStatus', 'pumpStatus'

)


pumpstatus=0

# Functions that are executed for each path.

class index:
```

```
    def GET(self):
        page = open("agro.html", "r").read()
        return page
class pumpOn:
    def GET(self):
        global pumpstatus
        pumpstatus=1
        data=web.input()
        os.system("sudo python relayon.py")
        return '<i class="fa fa-arrow-circle-
up"></i> Watering started!'
class pumpOff:
    def GET(self):
        global pumpstatus
        pumpstatus=0
        os.system("sudo python relayoff.py")
        return '<i class="fa fa-arrow-circle-
down"></i> Watering stoped!'

class pumpStatus:
    def GET(self):
        data={}
        data["status"]=pumpstatus
        return json.dumps(data)

class turnLiter:
    def GET(self):
        os.system("sudo python relayon.py")
        global pumpstatus
        pumpstatus=1
        data=web.input()
        return pulseEvent(data.liter)
```

```
#starting the server
if __name__ == "__main__":
    app = web.application(urls, globals())
    app.run()
    os.system("sudo python soilmoisture.py")
```

After finishing of typing the code, the file should be saved under the name **server.py**. Location to save the file on your computer can be any. In this case, the script is saved on the Desktop. If we are in the /home/pi folder, to start the script that is on the desktop, we need to enter the following two commands:

```
cd Desktop
sudo python server.py
```

After running these two commands Python program will start webserver. Ending the execution of program is done with Ctrl+C command.

10.3.4. All necessary codes for web application

```
<html>
<head>
<!-- Adjusting layout -->
<style type="text/css">
  .img-responsive {
    display: block;
    max-width: 100%;
    width: 100%;
    height: auto;
}
}
#bodylogin {
```

```
        text-align: center;
}
</style>
<!--Importing the necessary files -->
<link rel="stylesheet"
href="https://maxcdn.bootstrapcdn.com/bootstrap/
3.3.4/css/bootstrap.min.css">
<link rel="stylesheet"
href="//maxcdn.bootstrapcdn.com/font-
awesome/4.3.0/css/font-awesome.min.css">
<script
src="https://ajax.googleapis.com/ajax/libs/jquer
y/2.1.3/jquery.min.js"></script>
<script
src="https://cdn.jsdelivr.net/sweetalert2/3.2.3/
sweetalert2.min.js"></script>
<link rel="stylesheet"
href="https://cdn.jsdelivr.net/sweetalert2/3.2.3
/sweetalert2.css">

<meta charset="utf-8">
<meta http-equiv="X-UA-Compatible" con-
tent="IE=edge">
<meta name="viewport" content="width=device-
width, initial-scale=1">

<!-- Javascript to call a Web Server -->
<script type="text/javascript">
        var status;
        function pumpOn()
        {
```

```
$.get('http://192.168.0.22:8080/turnon, {},
function(data) {
                $('#showmessage').html(data);
                $('#but-
tonturnon').attr("disabled", true);
                $('#buttonFil-
ter').attr("disabled", true);
            });
        }
        function pumpOff()
        {


$.get('http://192.168.0.22:8080/turnoff, {},
function(data) {
                $('#showmessage').html(data);
                $('#but-
tonturnon').attr("disabled", false);
                $('#buttonFil-
ter').attr("disabled", false);
            });
        }


        function turnLiter()
        {
          var numliter = $("#numliter").val();
          if(numliter.length==0){
            swal(
                Error!',
                'Empty field...',
                'error'
              )
          } else {
```

```
        $("#buttonFil-
ter").button('loading');
        $('#but-
tonturnon').attr("disabled", true);
        $('#but-
tonturnoff').attr("disabled", true);


$.get('http://192.168.0.22:8080/turnLiter?liter=
'+numliter, {}, function(data) {
        $('#showmmessage').html("<i
class='fa fa-circle-o-notch fa-spin '></i> Wa-
tering by flow in progress...");
        checkStatusWhenFlow();
    });
    }
    }


    function pumpStatus() {

        $.getJSON(
"http://192.168.0.22:8080/pumpStatus", function(
json ) {
        status = json.status;
        });
        return parseInt(status);
        }


    function checkStatusWhenFlow () {
        tajmer = setInterval(function(){
          if(pumpStatus()==0) {
            clearInterval(tajmer);
```

```
                    $("#buttonFil-
ter").button('reset');
                $('#but-
tonturnon').attr("disabled", false);
                $('#but-
tonturnoff').attr("disabled", false);
                $('#numliter').val("");

$('#showmmessage').html("Waiting for input...");
                }
            }, 500);
        }



</script>
</head>
<!-- HTML section that displays forms used to
manage Web Server -->
<body id="body" >
    <a name="top"></a>
    <div class="container-fluid"
id="bodylogin">
        <div class="row" id="loginformadiv">
        <div class="col-lg-4 col-sm-4 col-xs-
12">

        </div>
        <div class="col-lg-4 col-sm-4 col-xs-
12">

        <h1><i class="fa fa-tint"></i> Smart
Agro Systems</h1>
        <div class="row">
        <div class="col-lg-12">
            <div id="showmmessage"
class="alert alert-info">SMART AGRO</div>
```

```
            </div>

            <div class="col-lg-6">
                <button class="btn btn-success
btn-block" id="buttonturnon" on-
click="pumpOn();"><i class="fa fa-arrow-circle-
up"></i> Turn on watering</button>
            </div>
                <div class="col-lg-6">
                <button class="btn btn-danger btn-
block" id="buttonturnoff" on-
click="pumpOff();"><i class="fa fa-arrow-circle-
down"></i> Turn off watering</button>
                </div>


            </div>
            <br>
            <hr>
            <div class="row">
                <div class="col-lg-12">
                    <div id="showmmessage2"
class="alert alert-info">Adjusting the
flow</div>
                </div>
                <div class="col-lg-12">
                    <div class="form-group">
                        <label
for="exampleInputEmail1">Enter the number of li-
ters</label>
                        <input type="text"
class="form-control" id="numliter"  placehold-
er="For example 1 or 0.5 liter">
```

```
          </div>
          <button class="btn btn-success
btn-block" id="buttonFilter" data-loading-
text="<i class='fa fa-circle-o-notch fa-spin
'></i> Processing..." onclick="turnLiter();"><i
class="fa fa-filter"></i> Turn on</button>
          </div>
        </div>
        </div>
        <div class="col-lg-4 col-sm-4 col-xs-
12">
        </div>
      </div>

      <script
src="https://maxcdn.bootstrapcdn.com/bootstrap/3
.3.4/js/bootstrap.min.js"></script>
</body>
</html>
```

After finishing of typing the code, the file should be saved under the name **agro.html** and stored on Raspberry Pi desktop.

Web application for Smart agriculture consists of 2 parts. The first part refers to turning on and of the watering. As for the second part, it represents a more advanced functionality where we can enter the desired amount of water (sent via GET parameter) to be verified by flow sensor. After clicking on the button "Turn on watering" all the buttons are blocked automatically except for the "Turn off watering" button that interrupts this command. Assigning and starting the flow of water all the buttons are blocked until the flow is over during the watering process, execution of functions are animated on web application.

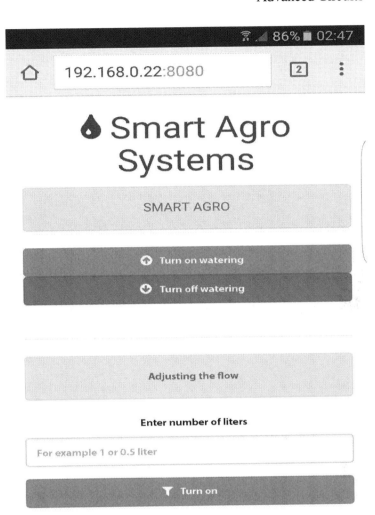

Image 21 Smart agriculture web application

About the Author

Thomas Charleston is a professional computer scientist with specialty in Computers, IT, and Programming. He is an author and prominent writer of non-fiction books in the science niche and the author of the "RASPBERRY PI 3:2016 USER GUIDE FOR BEGINNERS", "Raspberry PI3: Enchanted Guide for Starters". Thomas is mostly known for his ability to fix but simple and sophisticated issues with regards to the IT world. As a lover of technology, he sends most of his time research, carrying out experience and trying out new things.